This Travel Journal Belongs To:

AREA *Suggestions*

PLACES TO VISIT:

Orléans

Sancerre

Blois

Montrésor

Tours

Chinon

Saumur

Algers

Azay -le -Rideau

Beaugency

Amboise

Lavardin

Vendôme

Bourges

Loches

Nantes

LOIRE VALLEY WINE REGIONS:

Centre- Loire

Anjou and Saumur

Touraine and Vouvray

Pays Nantais

THINGS TO DO & SEE:

Loire Valley Wine Tours

Château de Chambord

Château de Chenonceau

Bourges Cathedral

Château de Brissac

Château d'Azay-le-Rideau

Château Royal d'Amboise

Château de Meung-sur-Loire & Château de Sully-Sur-Loire

Cathédrale Sainte-Croix d'Orléans

Château de Cheverny

Château de Villandry

Château d'Angers

Château du Clos Lucé & Leonardo's Garden

Musée des Blindés

Château de Brissac

Château d'Ussé

Château Royal de Blois

Abbaye de la Trinité de Vendôme

Musée des 24 Heures du Mans

Forteresse Royale de Chinon

LOIRE *Bucket List*

PLACES I WANT TO VISIT:

THINGS I WANT TO DO:

TOP 3 DESTINATIONS:

TRAVEL *Planner*

DESTINATION:

DATES:

BUDGET:

WEATHER:

CURRENCY EXCHANGE:

ACCOMODATION OVERVIEW

NAME:	LOCATION:	DATE:	ADDRESS:

NOTES & TRAVEL DETAILS

TRIP BUDGET *Planner*

TRIP DETAILS:

AMOUNT NEEDED:

OUR GOAL DATE:

DEPOSIT TRACKER

AMOUNT DEPOSITED: **DATE DEPOSITED:**

TRAVEL EXPENSE *Tracker*

DESTINATION: BUDGET GOAL:

DATE:	DESCRIPTION:	CURRENCY:	AMOUNT:

TOTAL EXPENSES:

TRAVEL EXPENSE *Tracker*

DESTINATION: _____   BUDGET GOAL: _____

DATE:	DESCRIPTION:	CURRENCY:	AMOUNT:

TOTAL EXPENSES:

FLIGHT *Information*

DATE: DESTINATION:

AIRLINE:	
BOOKING NUMBER:	
DEPARTURE DATE:	
BOARDING TIME:	
GATE NUMBER:	
SEAT NUMBER:	
FLIGHT DURATION:	
ARRIVAL / LANDING TIME:	

DATE: DESTINATION:

AIRLINE:	
BOOKING NUMBER:	
DEPARTURE DATE:	
BOARDING TIME:	
GATE NUMBER:	
SEAT NUMBER:	
FLIGHT DURATION:	
ARRIVAL / LANDING TIME:	

TRAIN *Information*

DATE: _____   DESTINATION: _____

TRAIN PASS (EURAIL, ETC.):	
DEPARTING STATION:	
DEPARTURE DATE:	
BOARDING TIME:	
GATE NUMBER:	
SEAT NUMBER:	
ARRIVAL STATION:	
ARRIVAL / LANDING TIME:	

DATE: _____   DESTINATION: _____

TRAIN PASS (EURAIL, ETC.):	
DEPARTING STATION:	
DEPARTURE DATE:	
BOARDING TIME:	
GATE NUMBER:	
SEAT NUMBER:	
ARRIVAL STATION:	
ARRIVAL / LANDING TIME:	

TRAIN *Information*

DATE: _____   DESTINATION: _____

TRAIN PASS (EURAIL, ETC.):	
DEPARTING STATION:	
DEPARTURE DATE:	
BOARDING TIME:	
GATE NUMBER:	
SEAT NUMBER:	
ARRIVAL STATION:	
ARRIVAL / LANDING TIME:	

DATE: _____   DESTINATION: _____

TRAIN PASS (EURAIL, ETC.):	
DEPARTING STATION:	
DEPARTURE DATE:	
BOARDING TIME:	
GATE NUMBER:	
SEAT NUMBER:	
ARRIVAL STATION:	
ARRIVAL / LANDING TIME:	

VEHICLE *Information*

TYPE: PERSONAL RENTAL

CAR RENTAL AGENCY:	
CONTACT INFORMATION:	
PICK UP DATE AND TIME:	
RETURN DATE AND TIME:	
MAKE & MODEL:	
INSPECTION NOTES:	
COST PER DAY:	
TOTAL COST:	

TYPE: GUIDED TOUR RENTAL

TOUR BUS RENTAL:	
TOUR COMPANY CONTACT:	
TOUR GUIDE NAME:	
DEPARTURE DATE AND TIME:	
LOCATIONS TO BE VISITED:	
COST PER TICKET:	
TOTAL COST FOR GROUP:	

TRAVEL *Planner*

PRE-TRAVEL CHECKLIST

1 MONTH BEFORE

☐
☐
☐
☐
☐

2 WEEKS BEFORE

☐
☐
☐
☐
☐

1 WEEK BEFORE

☐
☐
☐
☐
☐

2 DAYS BEFORE

☐
☐
☐
☐
☐

24 HOURS BEFORE

☐
☐
☐
☐
☐

DAY OF TRAVEL

☐
☐
☐
☐
☐

TRIP TO DO *List*

PACKING *Check List*

DOCUMENTS

- [ ] PASSPORT
- [ ] DRIVER'S LICENSE
- [ ] VISA
- [ ] PLANE TICKETS
- [ ] LOCAL CURRENCY
- [ ] INSURANCE CARD
- [ ] HEALTH CARD
- [ ] OTHER ID
- [ ] HOTEL INFO
- [ ] _____

CLOTHING

- [ ] SOCKS
- [ ] SWIM WEAR
- [ ] T-SHIRTS
- [ ] JEANS/PANTS
- [ ] SHORTS
- [ ] SKIRTS / DRESSES
- [ ] JACKET / COAT
- [ ] SLEEPWEAR
- [ ] SHOES
- [ ] _____

PERSONAL ITEMS

- [ ] SHAMPOO
- [ ] RAZORS
- [ ] COSMETICS
- [ ] HAIR BRUSH
- [ ] LIP BALM
- [ ] WATER BOTTLE
- [ ] SOAP
- [ ] TOOTHBRUSH
- [ ] JEWELRY
- [ ] _____

ELECTRONICS

- [ ] CELL PHONE
- [ ] CHARGER
- [ ] LAPTOP
- [ ] BATTERIES
- [ ] EARPHONES
- [ ] CAMERA
- [ ] MEMORY CARD
- [ ] _____
- [ ] _____
- [ ] _____

HEALTH & SAFETY

- [ ] HAND SANITIZER
- [ ] SUNSCREEN
- [ ] VITAMIN
- [ ] BANDAIDS
- [ ] ADVIL/TYLENOL
- [ ] GLASSES
- [ ] COLD/FLU MEDS
- [ ] _____
- [ ] _____
- [ ] _____

ESSENTIALS

- [ ] _____
- [ ] _____
- [ ] _____
- [ ] _____
- [ ] _____
- [ ] _____
- [ ] _____
- [ ] _____
- [ ] _____
- [ ] _____

PACKING *Check List*

DATE OF TRIP:

DURATION:

OUTFIT *Planner*

DAY: DESTINATION: PACKED: ☐

DAY: EVENING:

ACTIVITY:

OUTFIT:

SHOES:

ACC:

DAY: DESTINATION: PACKED: ☐

DAY: EVENING:

ACTIVITY:

OUTFIT:

SHOES:

ACC:

DAY: DESTINATION: PACKED: ☐

DAY: EVENING:

ACTIVITY:

OUTFIT:

SHOES:

ACC:

OUTFIT *Planner*

DAY: DESTINATION: PACKED:

DAY: EVENING:

ACTIVITY:

OUTFIT:

SHOES:

ACC:

DAY: DESTINATION: PACKED:

DAY: EVENING:

ACTIVITY:

OUTFIT:

SHOES:

ACC:

DAY: DESTINATION: PACKED:

DAY: EVENING:

ACTIVITY:

OUTFIT:

SHOES:

ACC:

OUTFIT *Planner*

DAY: DESTINATION: PACKED: ☐

DAY: EVENING:

ACTIVITY:

OUTFIT:

SHOES:

ACC:

DAY: DESTINATION: PACKED: ☐

DAY: EVENING:

ACTIVITY:

OUTFIT:

SHOES:

ACC:

DAY: DESTINATION: PACKED: ☐

DAY: EVENING:

ACTIVITY:

OUTFIT:

SHOES:

ACC:

OUTFIT *Planner*

DAY: DESTINATION: PACKED:

DAY: EVENING:

ACTIVITY:

OUTFIT:

SHOES:

ACC:

DAY: DESTINATION: PACKED:

DAY: EVENING:

ACTIVITY:

OUTFIT:

SHOES:

ACC:

DAY: DESTINATION: PACKED:

DAY: EVENING:

ACTIVITY:

OUTFIT:

SHOES:

ACC:

OUTFIT *Planner*

DAY: DESTINATION: PACKED: ☐

DAY: EVENING:

ACTIVITY:

OUTFIT:

SHOES:

ACC:

DAY: DESTINATION: PACKED: ☐

DAY: EVENING:

ACTIVITY:

OUTFIT:

SHOES:

ACC:

DAY: DESTINATION: PACKED: ☐

DAY: EVENING:

ACTIVITY:

OUTFIT:

SHOES:

ACC:

OUTFIT *Planner*

DAY: DESTINATION: PACKED: ☐

                 DAY: EVENING:

ACTIVITY:

OUTFIT:

SHOES:

ACC:

DAY: DESTINATION: PACKED: ☐

                 DAY: EVENING:

ACTIVITY:

OUTFIT:

SHOES:

ACC:

DAY: DESTINATION: PACKED: ☐

                 DAY: EVENING:

ACTIVITY:

OUTFIT:

SHOES:

ACC:

OUTFIT *Planner*

DAY: DESTINATION: PACKED: ☐

DAY: EVENING:

ACTIVITY:

OUTFIT:

SHOES:

ACC:

DAY: DESTINATION: PACKED: ☐

DAY: EVENING:

ACTIVITY:

OUTFIT:

SHOES:

ACC:

DAY: DESTINATION: PACKED: ☐

DAY: EVENING:

ACTIVITY:

OUTFIT:

SHOES:

ACC:

OUTFIT *Planner*

DAY: DESTINATION: PACKED: ☐

           DAY: EVENING:

ACTIVITY:

OUTFIT:

SHOES:

ACC:

DAY: DESTINATION: PACKED: ☐

           DAY: EVENING:

ACTIVITY:

OUTFIT:

SHOES:

ACC:

DAY: DESTINATION: PACKED: ☐

           DAY: EVENING:

ACTIVITY:

OUTFIT:

SHOES:

ACC:

TRAVEL *Checklist*

DESTINATION: CENTRE-LOIRE   DATES:

NOTABLE TOWNS

Orléans

Sancerre

Meung-sur-Loire

Beaugency

Gien

Nantes

POPULAR WINERIES

Bourgeois Henri Domaine

Cave Eric Louis - Celliers de la Pauline

Domaine Bernard Fleuriet et Fils

Domaine du Croc du Merle

POPULAR HOTELS

Hôtel Escale Oceania Orléans

THINGS TO DO

Winery Tours

Parc Floral de la Source

Cathédrale Sainte-Croix d'Orléans

Abbaye de Fleury

Château de Meung-sur-Loire

Château de Chamerolles

Château of Sully-sur-Loire

Explore by bike - Loire à Vélo

Hôtel Groslot d'Orléans

 Regional Wines: Sancerre & Pouilly-Fumé Sauvignon Blanc

TOP MUSEUMS

Musée des Beaux-Arts d'Orléans

Maison des Étangs

Musée Historique et Archéologique de l'Orléanais

HOTEL *Information*

NAME OF HOTEL:

ADDRESS:

PHONE NUMBER:

CONFIRMATION #:

CHECK IN/OUT:

ROOM TYPE:

RATE:

NAME OF HOTEL:

ADDRESS:

PHONE NUMBER:

CONFIRMATION #:

CHECK IN/OUT:

ROOM TYPE:

RATE:

NOTES

TRAVEL *Itinerary*

DESTINATION: DATE:

MON

TUE

WED

THU

FRI

SAT

SUN

VACATION *Planner*

DAILY ITINERARY

DATE: _____

LOCATION: _____

BUDGET: _____

TOP ACTIVITIES

MEAL PLANNER

TIME: SCHEDULE:

EXPENSES

TOTAL COST: _____

NOTES:

TRAVEL *Planner*

DATE: DAY:

☀ 🌤 🌦 ☁ ⛈

6

7

8

9

10

11   REMINDERS

12

1

2

3

4

5

6

7

8

9

10

11

12

VACATION *Planner*

DAILY ITINERARY

DATE: _____

LOCATION: _____

BUDGET: _____

TOP ACTIVITIES

MEAL PLANNER

TIME: SCHEDULE:

EXPENSES

TOTAL COST: _____

NOTES:

TRAVEL *Planner*

DATE: DAY:

NOTES

☀ ⛅ 🌦 ☁ ⛈

6

7

8

9

10

11   REMINDERS

12

1

2

3

4

5

6

7

8

9

10

11

12

TRAVEL *Notes*

DATE: LOCATION:

DATE: LOCATION:

TRAVEL *Journal*

DATE: _____

_____

_____

_____

_____

_____

_____

_____

_____

_____

_____

_____

_____

_____

_____

TRAVEL *Journal*

DATE: _____

_____

_____

_____

_____

_____

_____

_____

_____

_____

_____

_____

_____

_____

_____

WINE TASTING *Notes*

DATE: TOWN:

WINE NAME: **WINERY:**

TYPE OF GRAPE: **VINTAGE:**

APPEARANCE & SMELL:

TASTING NOTES: **FLORAL**   **CITRUS**   **WOODSY**   **SPICE**

PAIRING SUGGESTIONS:

FINAL RATING: ☆ ☆ ☆ ☆ ☆

TODAY'S FAVORITE MEMORIES:

WINE TASTING *Notes*

DATE: TOWN:

WINE NAME: **WINERY:**

TYPE OF GRAPE: **VINTAGE:**

APPEARANCE & SMELL:

TASTING NOTES: FLORAL   CITRUS   WOODSY   SPICE

PAIRING SUGGESTIONS:

FINAL RATING:

TODAY'S FAVORITE MEMORIES:

WINE TASTING *Notes*

DATE: TOWN:

WINE NAME: **WINERY:**

TYPE OF GRAPE: **VINTAGE:**

APPEARANCE & SMELL:

TASTING NOTES: **FLORAL   CITRUS   WOODSY   SPICE**

PAIRING SUGGESTIONS:

FINAL RATING: ☆ ☆ ☆ ☆ ☆

TODAY'S FAVORITE MEMORIES:

WINE TASTING *Notes*

DATE: TOWN:

WINE NAME: **WINERY:**

TYPE OF GRAPE: **VINTAGE:**

APPEARANCE & SMELL:

TASTING NOTES: **FLORAL   CITRUS   WOODSY   SPICE**

PAIRING SUGGESTIONS:

FINAL RATING: ☆ ☆ ☆ ☆ ☆

TODAY'S FAVORITE MEMORIES:

TRAVEL *Journal*

DATE: _____

TRAVEL *Journal*

DATE: _____

BEER TASTING *Notes*

DATE: TOWN:

BEER NAME: **BREWERY:**

TYPE OF HOPS: **TYPE OF BEER:**

APPEARANCE & BODY:

TASTING NOTES: HOPPY WOODSY CITRUS SOUR MALTY BITTER

PAIRING SUGGESTIONS:

FINAL RATING: ☆ ☆ ☆ ☆ ☆

TODAY'S FAVORITE MEMORIES:

BEER TASTING *Notes*

DATE: TOWN:

BEER NAME: **BREWERY:**

TYPE OF HOPS: **TYPE OF BEER:**

APPEARANCE & BODY:

TASTING NOTES: BITTER   HOPPY CITRUS SOUR   MALTY   FLORAL

PAIRING SUGGESTIONS:

FINAL RATING: ☆ ☆ ☆ ☆ ☆

TODAY'S FAVORITE MEMORIES:

TRAVEL *Journal*

DATE: _____

_____

_____

_____

_____

_____

_____

_____

_____

_____

_____

_____

_____

_____

_____

_____

TRAVEL *Journal*

DATE: _____

_____

_____

_____

_____

_____

_____

_____

_____

_____

_____

_____

_____

_____

_____

_____

TRAVEL *Checklist*

DESTINATION: Touraine - Vouvray   DATES:

POPULAR TOWNS

Tours

Blois

Amboise

Azay-le-Rideau

Vendôme

Valençay

POPULAR WINERIES

Les Caves du Père Auguste

Guillaume and Mathieu PLOU

Château de Minière

Domaine Huet - L'Échansonne

POPULAR HOTELS

Hôtel Le Pavillon des Lys

Hôtel Le Manoir Les Minimes

AREA CASTLES

Château de Chambord

Château de Chenonceau

Château de Cheverny

Château de Azay-Le-Rideau

Château de Villandry

Château d'Amboise

Château Royal de Blois

Château du Clos Lucé & Leonardo's Garden

Château d'Ussé

 Regional Wines:
Chenin Blanc, Sauvignon Blanc & Cabernet Franc

TO DO:

Jardin Botanique de Tours

Abbaye de la Trinité de Vendôme

Musée des 24 Heures du Mans

HOTEL *Information*

NAME OF HOTEL:

ADDRESS:

PHONE NUMBER:

CONFIRMATION #:

CHECK IN/OUT:

ROOM TYPE:

RATE:

NAME OF HOTEL:

ADDRESS:

PHONE NUMBER:

CONFIRMATION #:

CHECK IN/OUT:

ROOM TYPE:

RATE:

NOTES

TRAVEL *Itinerary*

DESTINATION: DATE:

MON

TUE

WED

THU

FRI

SAT

SUN

VACATION *Planner*

DAILY ITINERARY

DATE: _____

LOCATION: _____

BUDGET: _____

☀ ⛅ 🌦 ☁ ⛈

TOP ACTIVITIES

MEAL PLANNER

TIME: SCHEDULE:

EXPENSES

TOTAL COST: _____

NOTES:

TRAVEL *Planner*

DATE: _____

DAY: _____

NOTES

☀ ⛅ 🌦 ☁ ⛈

6 _____

7 _____

8 _____

9 _____

10 _____

11 _____

REMINDERS

12 _____

1 _____

2 _____

3 _____

4 _____

5 _____

6 _____

7 _____

8 _____

9 _____

10 _____

11 _____

12 _____

VACATION *Planner*

DAILY ITINERARY

DATE: _____

LOCATION: _____

BUDGET: _____

TOP ACTIVITIES

MEAL PLANNER

TIME: SCHEDULE:

EXPENSES

TOTAL COST: _____

NOTES:

TRAVEL *Planner*

DATE: DAY:

NOTES

6

7

8

9

10

11

REMINDERS

12

1

2

3

4

5

6

7

8

9

10

11

12

TRAVEL *Notes*

DATE: LOCATION:

DATE: LOCATION:

WINE TASTING *Notes*

DATE: TOWN:

WINE NAME: **WINERY:**

TYPE OF GRAPE: **VINTAGE:**

APPEARANCE & SMELL:

TASTING NOTES: **FLORAL   CITRUS   WOODSY   SPICY**

PAIRING SUGGESTIONS:

FINAL RATING: ☆ ☆ ☆ ☆ ☆

TODAY'S FAVORITE MEMORIES:

WINE TASTING *Notes*

DATE: TOWN:

WINE NAME: **WINERY:**

TYPE OF GRAPE: **VINTAGE:**

APPEARANCE & SMELL:

TASTING NOTES: **FLORAL   CITRUS   WOODSY   SPICE**

PAIRING SUGGESTIONS:

FINAL RATING:

TODAY'S FAVORITE MEMORIES:

WINE TASTING *Notes*

DATE: TOWN:

WINE NAME: **WINERY:**

TYPE OF GRAPE: **VINTAGE:**

APPEARANCE & SMELL:

TASTING NOTES: **FLORAL   CITRUS   WOODSY   SPICE**

PAIRING SUGGESTIONS:

FINAL RATING: ☆ ☆ ☆ ☆ ☆

TODAY'S FAVORITE MEMORIES:

WINE TASTING *Notes*

DATE: TOWN:

WINE NAME: **WINERY:**

TYPE OF GRAPE: **VINTAGE:**

APPEARANCE & SMELL:

TASTING NOTES: **FLORAL   CITRUS   WOODSY   SPICE**

PAIRING SUGGESTIONS:

FINAL RATING: ☆ ☆ ☆ ☆ ☆

TODAY'S FAVORITE MEMORIES:

TRAVEL *Journal*

DATE: _____

_____

_____

_____

_____

_____

_____

_____

_____

_____

_____

_____

_____

_____

_____

_____

TRAVEL *Journal*

DATE: _____

_____

_____

_____

_____

_____

_____

_____

_____

_____

_____

_____

_____

_____

_____

_____

TRAVEL *Journal*

DATE: _____

Bon Voyage

WINE TASTING *Notes*

DATE: TOWN:

WINE NAME: **WINERY:**

TYPE OF GRAPE: **VINTAGE:**

APPEARANCE & SMELL:

TASTING NOTES: **FLORAL   CITRUS   WOODSY   SPICE**

PAIRING SUGGESTIONS:

FINAL RATING: ☆ ☆ ☆ ☆ ☆

TODAY'S FAVORITE MEMORIES:

WINE TASTING *Notes*

DATE: TOWN:

WINE NAME: **WINERY:**

TYPE OF GRAPE: **VINTAGE:**

APPEARANCE & SMELL:

TASTING NOTES: **FLORAL   CITRUS   WOODSY   SPICE**

PAIRING SUGGESTIONS:

FINAL RATING:

TODAY'S FAVORITE MEMORIES:

TRAVEL *Journal*

DATE: _____

TRAVEL *Journal*

DATE: _____

TRAVEL *Checklist*

DESTINATION: Anjou - Saumur   **DATES:**

NOTABLE TOWNS

Saumur

Angers

Anjour

Chinon

Montsoreau

Candes-Saint-Martin

POPULAR WINERIES

Bouvet Ladubay

Domaine Pierre et Bertrand Couly

Les Vins Domaine du Closel Château des Vaults

Le Domaine des Vallettes

POPULAR HOTELS

Au Relais Saint Maurice

Le Prieuré

THINGS TO DO

Château de Saumur

The Royal Fortress of Chinon & Cité Médiéval

Château de Brissac

Musée des Blindés

Musée Jean-Lurçat

Musée des Beaux-Arts d'Angers

Parc Naturel Régional Loire-Anjou-Touraine

Château de Charmont

Cathédrale Saint-Maurice d'Angers

 Regional Wines:
Chenin blanc, rosé, and Sparkling wines

WHERE TO EAT

LAIT THYM SEL

Gambetta

Le Pot de Lapin

HOTEL *Information*

HOTEL INFORMATION

NAME OF HOTEL:

ADDRESS:

PHONE NUMBER:

CONFIRMATION #:

CHECK IN/OUT:

ROOM TYPE:

RATE:

HOTEL INFORMATION

NAME OF HOTEL:

ADDRESS:

PHONE NUMBER:

CONFIRMATION #:

CHECK IN/OUT:

ROOM TYPE:

RATE:

NOTES

TRAVEL *Itinerary*

DESTINATION: DATE:

MON

TUE

WED

THU

FRI

SAT

SUN

VACATION *Planner*

DAILY ITINERARY

DATE: _____

LOCATION: _____

BUDGET: _____

TOP ACTIVITIES

MEAL PLANNER

TIME: SCHEDULE:

EXPENSES

TOTAL COST: _____

NOTES:

TRAVEL *Planner*

DATE:

DAY:

NOTES

☀ ⛅ 🌦 ☁ ⛈

REMINDERS

6

7

8

9

10

11

12

1

2

3

4

5

6

7

8

9

10

11

12

TRAVEL *Planner*

DATE: _____   DAY: _____

☀ ⛅ 🌧 ☁ ⛈

NOTES

6

7

8

9

10

11   REMINDERS

12

1

2

3

4

5

6

7

8

9

10

11

12

TRAVEL *Notes*

DATE: LOCATION:

DATE: LOCATION:

WINE TASTING *Notes*

DATE:

TOWN:

WINE NAME:

WINERY:

TYPE OF GRAPE:

VINTAGE:

APPEARANCE & SMELL:

TASTING NOTES:　　　　**FLORAL　　CITRUS　　WOODSY　　SPICE**

PAIRING SUGGESTIONS:

FINAL RATING:　☆　☆　☆　☆　☆

TODAY'S FAVORITE MEMORIES:

WINE TASTING *Notes*

DATE: TOWN:

WINE NAME: **WINERY:**

TYPE OF GRAPE: **VINTAGE:**

APPEARANCE & SMELL:

TASTING NOTES: **FLORAL   CITRUS   WOODSY   SPICE**

PAIRING SUGGESTIONS:

FINAL RATING: ☆ ☆ ☆ ☆ ☆

TODAY'S FAVORITE MEMORIES:

WINE TASTING *Notes*

DATE: TOWN:

WINE NAME: **WINERY:**

TYPE OF GRAPE: **VINTAGE:**

APPEARANCE & SMELL:

TASTING NOTES: **FLORAL   CITRUS   WOODSY   SPICE**

PAIRING SUGGESTIONS:

FINAL RATING:

TODAY'S FAVORITE MEMORIES:

WINE TASTING *Notes*

DATE: TOWN:

WINE NAME: **WINERY:**

TYPE OF GRAPE: **VINTAGE:**

APPEARANCE & SMELL:

TASTING NOTES: **FLORAL   CITRUS   WOODSY   SPICE**

PAIRING SUGGESTIONS:

FINAL RATING: ☆ ☆ ☆ ☆ ☆

TODAY'S FAVORITE MEMORIES:

TRAVEL *Journal*

DATE: _____

WINE TASTING *Notes*

DATE: TOWN:

WINE NAME: **WINERY:**

TYPE OF GRAPE: **VINTAGE:**

APPEARANCE & SMELL:

TASTING NOTES: FLORAL   CITRUS   WOODSY   SPICE

PAIRING SUGGESTIONS:

FINAL RATING: ☆ ☆ ☆ ☆ ☆

TODAY'S FAVORITE MEMORIES:

WINE TASTING *Notes*

DATE: TOWN:

WINE NAME: **WINERY:**

TYPE OF GRAPE: **VINTAGE:**

APPEARANCE & SMELL:

TASTING NOTES: **FLORAL   CITRUS   WOODSY   SPICE**

PAIRING SUGGESTIONS:

FINAL RATING: ☆ ☆ ☆ ☆ ☆

TODAY'S FAVORITE MEMORIES:

TRAVEL *Journal*

DATE: _____

_____

_____

_____

_____

_____

_____

_____

_____

_____

_____

_____

_____

_____

travel is always a good IDEA

TRAVEL *Journal*

DATE: _____

_____

_____

_____

_____

_____

_____

_____

_____

_____

_____

_____

_____

_____

Bon Voyage

TRAVEL *Journal*

DATE: _____

_____

_____

_____

_____

_____

_____

_____

_____

_____

_____

_____

_____

TRAVEL *Journal*

DATE: _____

TRAVEL *Journal*

DATE: _____

TRAVEL *Checklist*

DESTINATION: Pays Nantais   DATES:

NOTABLE TOWNS

Nantes

Trentemoult

Clisson

THINGS TO DO

Winery Tours

Nantes Cathedral

Les Machines de l'île

Château des Ducs de Bretagne

Musée d'Histoire de Nantes

Passage Pomeraye

Jardin des Plantes

Musée d'Arts de Nantes

Excursion to Vannes or Noirmoutier Island

POPULAR WINERIES

Domaine Courier

Vignoble Marchais - Le Chai de Thouaré sur Loire

The Castle of the Cassemichère

Domaine de la Foliette

 Regional Wine: Muscadet or Melon de Bourgogne

WHERE TO EAT

Le Reflet

Pickles

Restaurant L'Atlantide 1874 - Maison Guého

POPULAR HOTELS

Hôtel Oceania Hôtel de France

OKKO HOTELS Nantes Château

HOTEL *Information*

NAME OF HOTEL:

ADDRESS:

PHONE NUMBER:

CONFIRMATION #:

CHECK IN/OUT:

ROOM TYPE:

RATE:

NAME OF HOTEL:

ADDRESS:

PHONE NUMBER:

CONFIRMATION #:

CHECK IN/OUT:

ROOM TYPE:

RATE:

NOTES

TRAVEL *Itinerary*

DESTINATION: DATE:

MON

TUE

WED

THU

FRI

SAT

SUN

VACATION *Planner*

DAILY ITINERARY

DATE: _____

LOCATION: _____

BUDGET: _____

TOP ACTIVITIES

MEAL PLANNER

TIME: SCHEDULE:

EXPENSES

TOTAL COST: _____

NOTES:

TRAVEL *Planner*

DATE: DAY:

NOTES

6

7

8

9

10

11

REMINDERS

12

1

2

3

4

5

6

7

8

9

10

11

12

TRAVEL *Planner*

DATE:

DAY:

NOTES

☀ ⛅ 🌦 ☁ ⛈

REMINDERS

6

7

8

9

10

11

12

1

2

3

4

5

6

7

8

9

10

11

12

TRAVEL *Notes*

DATE: LOCATION:

DATE: LOCATION:

WINE TASTING *Notes*

DATE:

TOWN:

WINE NAME:

WINERY:

TYPE OF GRAPE:

VINTAGE:

APPEARANCE & SMELL:

TASTING NOTES: **FLORAL**   **CITRUS**   **WOODSY**   **SPICE**

PAIRING SUGGESTIONS:

FINAL RATING: ☆ ☆ ☆ ☆ ☆

TODAY'S FAVORITE MEMORIES:

WINE TASTING *Notes*

DATE: TOWN:

WINE NAME: **WINERY:**

TYPE OF GRAPE: **VINTAGE:**

APPEARANCE & SMELL:

TASTING NOTES: FLORAL   CITRUS   WOODSY   SPICE

PAIRING SUGGESTIONS:

FINAL RATING: ☆ ☆ ☆ ☆ ☆

TODAY'S FAVORITE MEMORIES:

WINE TASTING *Notes*

DATE: TOWN:

WINE NAME: **WINERY:**

TYPE OF GRAPE: **VINTAGE:**

APPEARANCE & SMELL:

TASTING NOTES: **FLORAL   CITRUS   WOODSY   SPICE**

PAIRING SUGGESTIONS:

FINAL RATING:

TODAY'S FAVORITE MEMORIES:

WINE TASTING *Notes*

DATE: TOWN:

WINE NAME: **WINERY:**

TYPE OF GRAPE: **VINTAGE:**

APPEARANCE & SMELL:

TASTING NOTES: **FLORAL   CITRUS   WOODSY   SPICE**

PAIRING SUGGESTIONS:

FINAL RATING:

TODAY'S FAVORITE MEMORIES:

WINE TASTING *Notes*

DATE: TOWN:

WINE NAME: **WINERY:**

TYPE OF GRAPE: **VINTAGE:**

APPEARANCE & SMELL:

TASTING NOTES: **FLORAL   CITRUS   WOODSY   SPICE**

PAIRING SUGGESTIONS:

FINAL RATING: ☆ ☆ ☆ ☆ ☆

TODAY'S FAVORITE MEMORIES:

WINE TASTING *Notes*

DATE: TOWN:

WINE NAME: **WINERY:**

TYPE OF GRAPE: **VINTAGE:**

APPEARANCE & SMELL:

TASTING NOTES: **FLORAL   CITRUS   WOODSY   SPICE**

PAIRING SUGGESTIONS:

FINAL RATING: ☆ ☆ ☆ ☆ ☆

TODAY'S FAVORITE MEMORIES:

TRAVEL *Journal*

DATE: _____

_____

_____

_____

_____

_____

_____

_____

_____

_____

_____

_____

_____

_____

_____

_____

_____

TRAVEL *Journal*

DATE: _____

TRAVEL *Journal*

DATE: _____

_____

_____

_____

_____

_____

_____

_____

_____

_____

_____

_____

_____

_____

_____

_____

Bon Voyage

TRAVEL *Checklist*

DESTINATION: DATES:

POPULAR HOTELS

THINGS TO DO

POPULAR WINERIES

RECOMMENDATIONS

WHERE TO EAT & DRINK

VACATION *Planner*

DAILY ITINERARY

DATE: _____

LOCATION: _____

BUDGET: _____

TOP ACTIVITIES

☀ ⛅ 🌦 ☁ ⛈

MEAL PLANNER

TIME: SCHEDULE:

EXPENSES

TOTAL COST: _____

NOTES:

TRAVEL *Planner*

DATE:

DAY:

NOTES

☀ ⛅ 🌧 ☁ ⛈

6

7

8

9

10

11

12

1

2

3

4

5

6

7

8

9

10

11

12

REMINDERS

TRAVEL *Journal*

DATE: _____

WINE TASTING *Notes*

DATE: TOWN:

WINE NAME: WINERY:

TYPE OF GRAPE: VINTAGE:

APPEARANCE & SMELL:

TASTING NOTES: FLORAL   CITRUS   WOODSY   SPICE

PAIRING SUGGESTIONS:

FINAL RATING: ☆ ☆ ☆ ☆ ☆

TODAY'S FAVORITE MEMORIES:

WINE TASTING *Notes*

DATE: **TOWN:**

WINE NAME: **WINERY:**

TYPE OF GRAPE: **VINTAGE:**

APPEARANCE & SMELL:

TASTING NOTES: FLORAL   CITRUS   WOODSY   SPICE

PAIRING SUGGESTIONS:

FINAL RATING: ☆ ☆ ☆ ☆ ☆

TODAY'S FAVORITE MEMORIES:

WINE TASTING *Notes*

DATE: TOWN:

WINE NAME: **WINERY:**

TYPE OF GRAPE: **VINTAGE:**

APPEARANCE & SMELL:

TASTING NOTES: FLORAL   CITRUS   WOODSY   SPICE

PAIRING SUGGESTIONS:

FINAL RATING: ☆ ☆ ☆ ☆ ☆

TODAY'S FAVORITE MEMORIES:

WINE TASTING *Notes*

DATE: TOWN:

WINE NAME: **WINERY:**

TYPE OF GRAPE: **VINTAGE:**

APPEARANCE & SMELL:

TASTING NOTES: **FLORAL   CITRUS   WOODSY   SPICE**

PAIRING SUGGESTIONS:

FINAL RATING: ☆ ☆ ☆ ☆ ☆

TODAY'S FAVORITE MEMORIES:

TRAVEL *Journal*

DATE: _____

TRAVEL *Journal*

DATE: _____

Enjoy
every
moment

TRAVEL *Checklist*

DESTINATION: DATES:

POPULAR HOTELS

THINGS TO DO

POPULAR WINERIES

RECOMMENDATIONS

WHERE TO EAT & DRINK

HOTEL *Information*

HOTEL INFORMATION

NAME OF HOTEL:

ADDRESS:

PHONE NUMBER:

CONFIRMATION #:

CHECK IN/OUT:

ROOM TYPE:

RATE:

HOTEL INFORMATION

NAME OF HOTEL:

ADDRESS:

PHONE NUMBER:

CONFIRMATION #:

CHECK IN/OUT:

ROOM TYPE:

RATE:

NOTES

TRAVEL *Itinerary*

DESTINATION: DATE:

MON

TUE

WED

THU

FRI

SAT

SUN

VACATION *Planner*

DAILY ITINERARY

DATE: _____

LOCATION: _____

BUDGET: _____

TOP ACTIVITIES

MEAL PLANNER

TIME: SCHEDULE:

EXPENSES

TOTAL COST: _____

NOTES:

TRAVEL *Planner*

DATE: DAY:

NOTES

6

7

8

9

10

11

REMINDERS

12

1

2

3

4

5

6

7

8

9

10

11

12

TRAVEL *Planner*

DATE: DAY:

NOTES

☀ 🌤 🌧 ☁ ⛈

6

7

8

9

10

11   REMINDERS

12

1

2

3

4

5

6

7

8

9

10

11

12

TRAVEL *Notes*

DATE: LOCATION:

DATE: LOCATION:

WINE TASTING *Notes*

DATE: TOWN:

WINE NAME: **WINERY:**

TYPE OF GRAPE: **VINTAGE:**

APPEARANCE & SMELL:

TASTING NOTES: **FLORAL**   **CITRUS**   **WOODSY**   **SPICE**

PAIRING SUGGESTIONS:

FINAL RATING: ☆ ☆ ☆ ☆ ☆

TODAY'S FAVORITE MEMORIES:

WINE TASTING *Notes*

DATE: TOWN:

WINE NAME: **WINERY:**

TYPE OF GRAPE: **VINTAGE:**

APPEARANCE & SMELL:

TASTING NOTES: **FLORAL   CITRUS   WOODSY   SPICE**

PAIRING SUGGESTIONS:

FINAL RATING: ☆ ☆ ☆ ☆ ☆

TODAY'S FAVORITE MEMORIES:

WINE TASTING *Notes*

DATE: TOWN:

WINE NAME: **WINERY:**

TYPE OF GRAPE: **VINTAGE:**

APPEARANCE & SMELL:

TASTING NOTES: FLORAL   CITRUS   WOODSY   SPICE

PAIRING SUGGESTIONS:

FINAL RATING: ☆ ☆ ☆ ☆ ☆

TODAY'S FAVORITE MEMORIES:

WINE TASTING *Notes*

DATE: TOWN:

WINE NAME: **WINERY:**

TYPE OF GRAPE: **VINTAGE:**

APPEARANCE & SMELL:

TASTING NOTES: FLORAL   CITRUS   WOODSY   SPICE

PAIRING SUGGESTIONS:

FINAL RATING: ☆ ☆ ☆ ☆ ☆

TODAY'S FAVORITE MEMORIES:

TRAVEL *Journal*

DATE: _____

TRAVEL *Journal*

DATE: _____

_____

_____

_____

_____

_____

_____

_____

_____

_____

_____

_____

_____

_____

TRAVEL *Journal*

DATE: _____

_____

_____

_____

_____

_____

_____

_____

_____

_____

_____

_____

_____

_____

_____

TRAVEL *Journal*

DATE: _____

_____

_____

_____

_____

_____

_____

_____

_____

_____

_____

_____

_____

_____

_____

_____

Made in United States
North Haven, CT
19 June 2022

20418796R00083